ramblings

a journey in poetry

e.p. rose
paintings by david burk

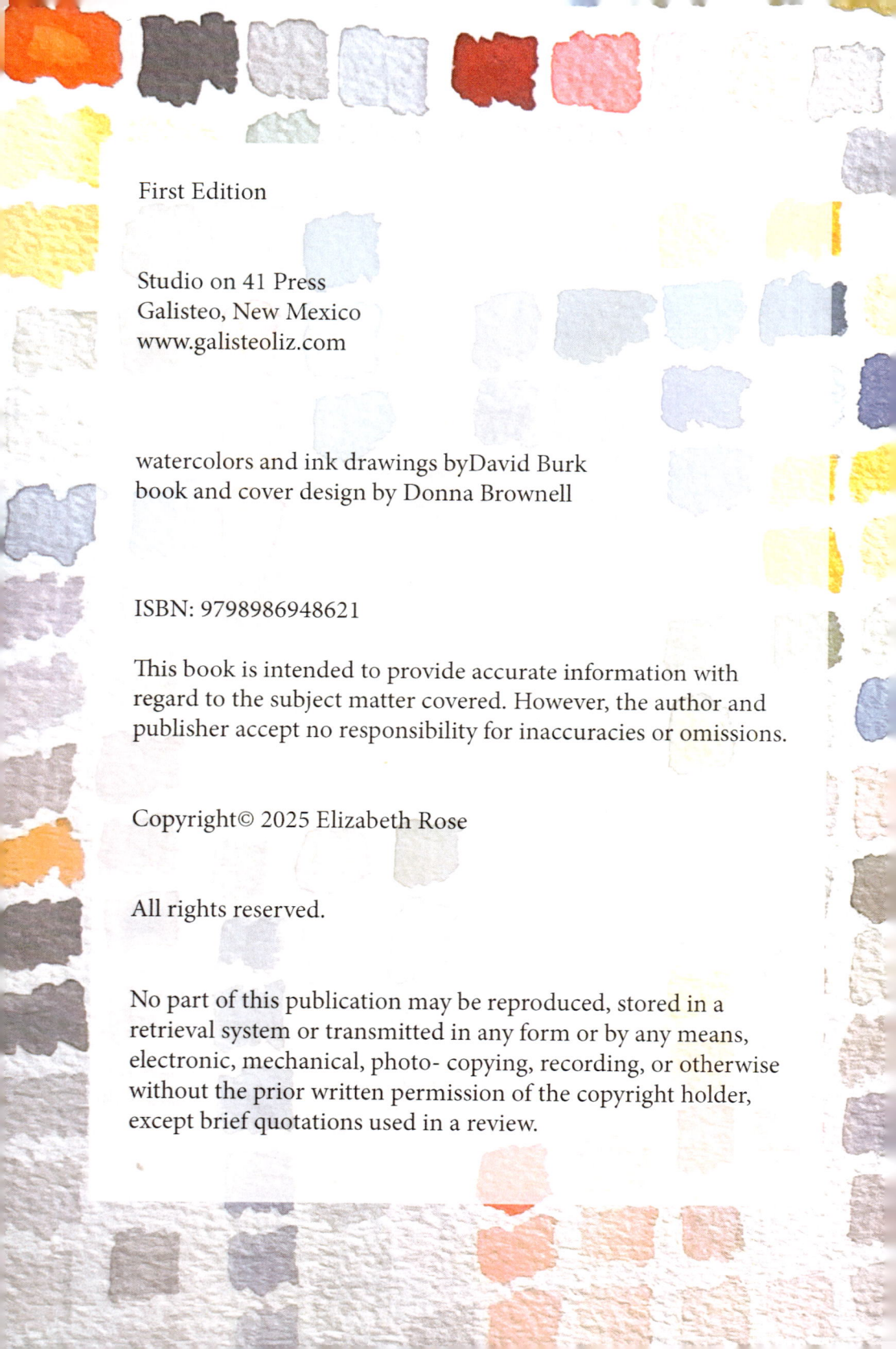

First Edition

Studio on 41 Press
Galisteo, New Mexico
www.galisteoliz.com

watercolors and ink drawings byDavid Burk
book and cover design by Donna Brownell

ISBN: 9798986948621

This book is intended to provide accurate information with regard to the subject matter covered. However, the author and publisher accept no responsibility for inaccuracies or omissions.

for Donna and those special beings who bring color to this world

who gifts me...?

unbidden the pencil
in my hand
penning thoughts not
thought by me
a tumbling
jumbling
waterfall
of words
surprise me
with a poem

contents

who decides

behind my house
a gate swings useless
from the broken fence post
give a little push and it gaps wide
enough for me to step through tread
dirt no different from the patch surrounding
the desert home I claim   *no trespassing allowed*
the fence wire warns though coyote on his hunt for
prey derides the delineation with his scat   following the
unbroken line-evidence of his nocturnal exploring   I came across
a dangling papery overcoat discarded on a rock in the arroyo by a rattler
a place where heel-toe imprints left by cottontails and leaping jackalope
pattern the sand   each day I walk the walk I walked yesterday
the walk I walked the day before   jumbled footprints
prove our nomadic desert comings   our daily goings
mocking ownership   last night the wind blew hard
erasing all existence of mine   of yours

I must hurry now to that place

how to describe a place
that exists solely in the depths
of
nothing   and   of THAT
a place of nothingness I can visit anytime
if
I turn the door handle to that place
I know rests eternally within my heart
know
when I reach there
know
it is nothing I will become

before Parkinson's

before Parkinson's
like love we made words together
quietly turning pages of our lives

before Parkinson's
scrambled soundtracks in his brain

before questions
hung unanswered and the roar of
television's tidal wave swept him away

like love
we used to make words together
before Parkinson's

a bridge

half-light hour
when   trees shape-shift to people
I walk the leafy lane to the wooden bridge
stare at its empty invitation

listen to the water's flow
watch its grey mass glide below
my feet hold firm   I cannot cross

air moist from the river bed cools my cheek
still I cannot cross

on the other side behind the stand of trees
the moon rises from her bed   dispels her shadows
extends a beam for me to grasp
I cannot reach it

a cloud appears   erases light
and with it my courage
retracing my steps
the way I'd come

I skipped home whistling

visitor from outer space

maple leaf jaunty in his hatband   *hello* said the visitor from Canada
hello and welcome   answered we   and we did   welcome him that is
and led him
to a trail of peanut butter ending at the open jar disguised but not too
well amongst the squash blossoms and pendulous vegetables we'd been
nursing for his visit

but we should have known

cucumbers   lettuce   sprouted cress were rabbit food to the city boy
rendered unclean by kangaroo mice midnight feastings   and   dainty
tooth-scars of their nibblings
I opened a packet of frozen peas to please him

next day we took him on a picnic   no ordinary picnic   a fancy three-
course affair all trimmings included and   some jolly fun   fun for us
that is   not fun for him as it turned out   who cared not one jot for
rock dwellings   the ancient kivas we'd taken him to see
he cleaned his red plastic plate before ours touched the gingham table

cloth spread French-style with glasses and a bottle of fermented grape wine while we still rolled Moroccan olives between our lips and spat pits into the grass and double-dipped chips in fiery salsa and sucked in the heady scent of pine through flared nostrils like stallions scenting a mare in season

not he

our guest was searching for a second can of fizzy diet soda and while dismembering the cold chicken with the tiger claws he used for hands checking   re-checking his watch *the football game kicks off in two minutes* he announced scraping the leftovers from his plate indicating he'd had enough before we'd carved the chicken or tossed the salad

back home

his eyeballs squared readied to receive touchdowns from the television 100 miles away from where we sat entranced by the water-song of tumbling river stones   the sunlight playing on the cottonwood leaves   us and everything it fingered

I don't think he liked us much I said

lunch at chows

The moon is hollow, the man at the restaurant table next to mine leaned towards his lunch companion *But you know that, of course* he said red-striped tie brushing the calamari on his plate.
Well, his companion nodded *You never see the other side of the moon, now do you? They…*he emphasized *never show you its far side do they, ever.*

Not quite following his logic, selecting a grain of rice and clamping it between my two chopsticks, I concentrated on guiding the morsel to my mouth to keep my neighbors from guessing I was hanging on their every word,

My two lunch girlfriends, Ellen and Joan, continued chatting assuming I was just too busy eating to talk. I tapped Ellen's arm—interrupt-

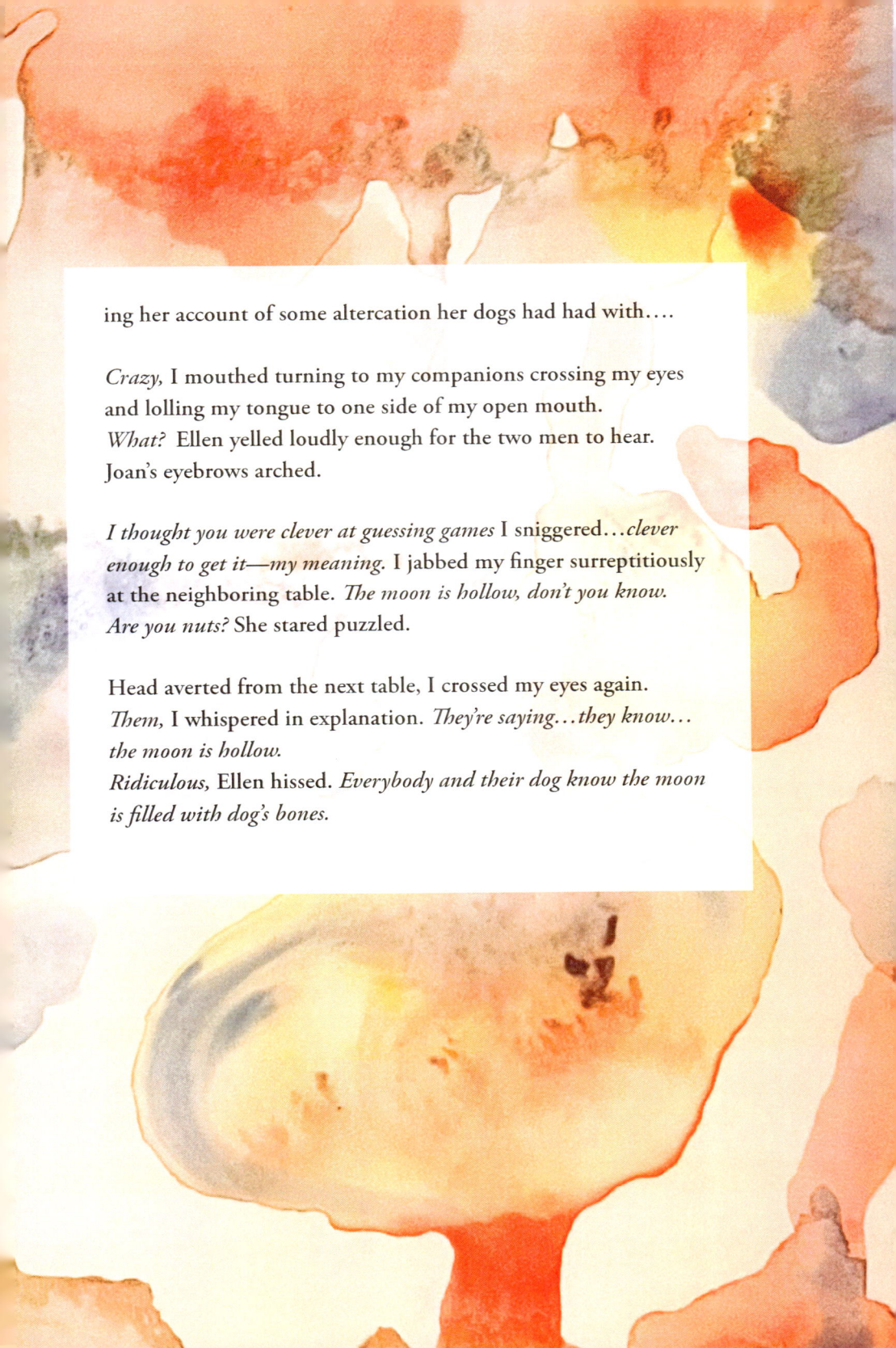

ing her account of some altercation her dogs had had with....

Crazy, I mouthed turning to my companions crossing my eyes
and lolling my tongue to one side of my open mouth.
What? Ellen yelled loudly enough for the two men to hear.
Joan's eyebrows arched.

I thought you were clever at guessing games I sniggered...*clever
enough to get it—my meaning.* I jabbed my finger surreptitiously
at the neighboring table. *The moon is hollow, don't you know.
Are you nuts?* She stared puzzled.

Head averted from the next table, I crossed my eyes again.
Them, I whispered in explanation. *They're saying...they know...
the moon is hollow.*
Ridiculous, Ellen hissed. *Everybody and their dog know the moon
is filled with dog's bones.*

maybe he listens

maybe   the woman's haunting
Sanskrit prayers carried by whisps
of *champa* incense
slip beneath his
bedroom door

where

he lies
and has for
thirteen nights
for thirteen days unmoving

maybe
her ringing notes gives him pause
rouse him to ponder his place
in the universe

maybe he sighs
maybe smiles
before he flies
maybe

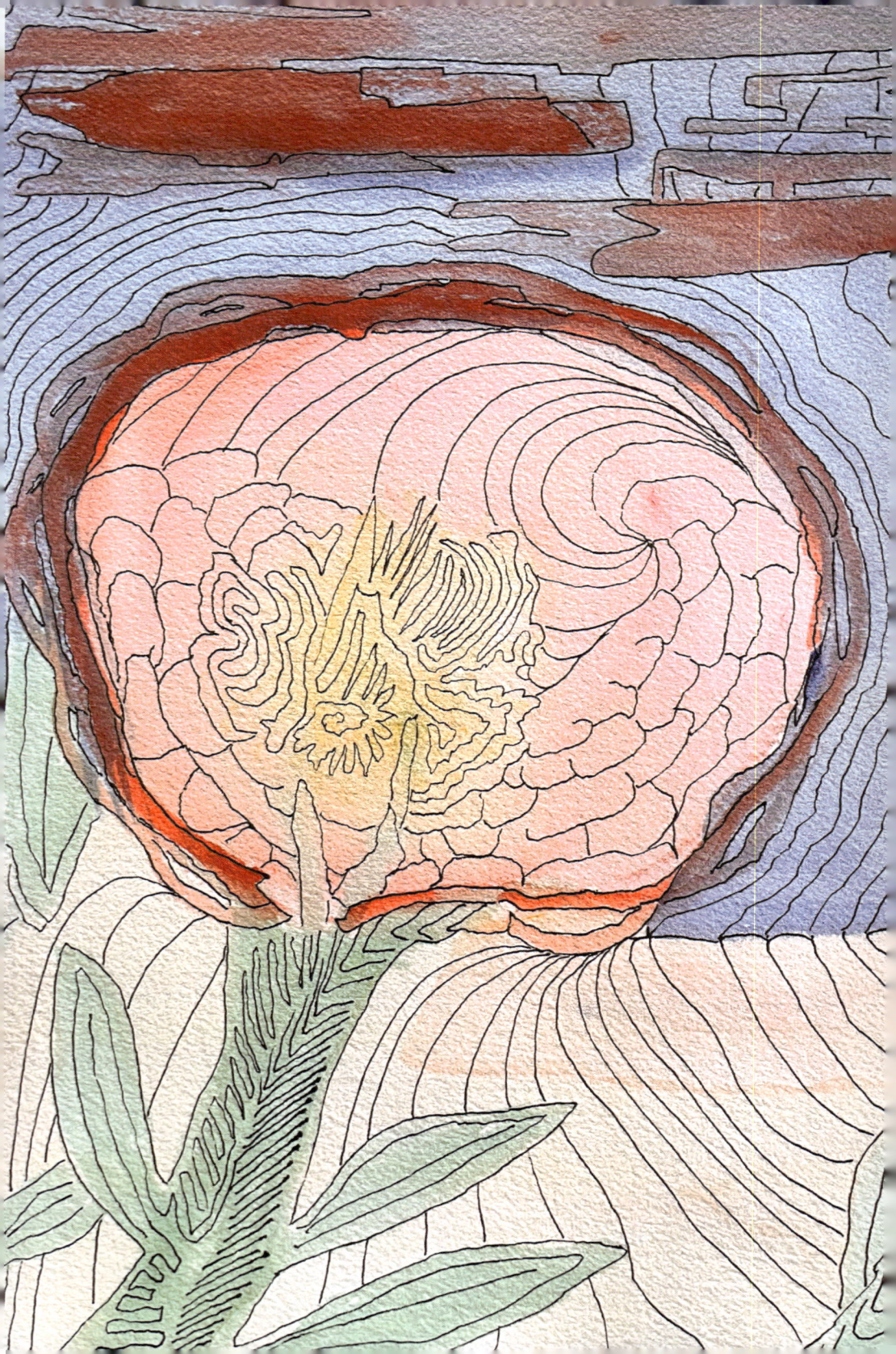

no birdsong I grieve for all you refugees

It's just a picture   one artist's image of the future I convince myself
push the treeless landscape from my mind   a world   where
warplanes etch a blackboard sky

no nighthawk sings
above me in the dark
I find no stars to map my path to sleep

a soundless scream escapes

it is me   the clouds of helicopters heat-seek   me
they aim to ensnare in their searchlight web
I sprint for cover   press my body against cold steel pray to be invisible

running low   no paper   no bag   no gun to weight my back
I hopscotch silver light pools   become a stag   leap the trip wires
hidden in the grass   shake off my pursuers
arrive no place   leave no shadow   wake sweating

to calm   I walk into to my garden   stare into
the dancing branches of the solitary elm
deep-breathe damp rain not yet arrived
listen   scan the night

whiplash wind stings   a serrated leaf blows against my boot
six raindrops wet my cheeks   the elm stills
no barn owl hoots his warning
I know the storm has come

coming in waves

its coming in waves and I don't like it
its dark so dark in this unknown sea
higher   faster I rise and sink
I soar and fall to the whim of the waves
pull   pull me   I call
and my daughters take my hands
but they can only comfort   no longer hold me
from the suffocating depths
which fill my eyes and ears till I lose sense of who I am

suddenly I am floating away from earth from all I know
to where I wot not nor want to be
pull   pull I try to cry but no voice comes
and I am alone riding the crest of my terror

forced to release my hold I slide
slip down a mighty wave
help   I cry but my mouth spills only ether
when in the dark a speck appears
tiny   bright   and all at once I'm beyond my dying
in a place of light and love peopled with all who ever loved me

I am home

red racers up on the hill

faces pressed
close against our
bedroom windowpane
we catch a sudden flash of red
fire the oak tree's shade in the yard
swaying to some inner dance of his alone
red racer rises on his tail   eyes fix on the blush-pink
object of his passion stretched in the sun along the wall
fecund   voluptuous   indifferent
ten feet from him her courtier
a surge of desire whiplashes him across the divide
lightly he brushes his skin to hers
streaks to his lookout post beneath the tree

again again   tongue flicking   sentinel   pulls full height
hurls through the air to her side
lazily she turns her head   tongue flickering her beckoning
tip to tip   belly to belly   together lie motionless   his at last

slithering   sliding   undulations speed to writhing
waves of their entwining

we could spy no more
hot breath steamed glass
falling backwards on the bed
our cheeks flushed red racer red

bombay. april 14 1944
two days after I turned six

a birthday party floats to view   mine
who the children were   or   what dress I wore   long forgotten

brown toast   butter dripping   salty heaven   I well remember
when halfway to my mouth   whoosh   a brown-winged thief
streaks through the open-sided   no-Indians-British-only teahouse
snatches it from my fingers   streams into the sky   I'm about to cry

look, look missy   uniformed   a bearer distracts   *see   cake coming*

chocolate cottage   icingsugar rambling roses frame a sugar
Snow White   pink-cheeked poised in the doorway matching
bluebird-blue dress to the pair of bluebirds in her hand

a cake too beautiful to eat
I have no words as its fairy-tale scene is set before me
there   and there   and there   I count seven pixies
in the windows   chimney   candle-lit roof
their pointy hats glow cochineal red

happy birthday   *make a wish missy-sahib*
gentle   the bearer wraps my hand about
the cake knife   pushes with me
lips puckered   summoning my secret wish
I lean towards six flickering flames   when

boom and *boom*
Bombay harbor mushrooms
to the sky   obliterates the sun   for
the minutest of moments sound suspends
the floor I stand on lifts a fraction beneath my feet
bangs   whistles   explosions releasing rainbow fire balls
shred the skyline   splinter black   splinter day
birthday cake   cast   race forgotten
children ayahs mothers servants my brother me scurry to the
railings
red gold silver blinding colored lights   myriads of stars arc mile-
high…
my best birthday surprise ever   my firework show   put on especially
for me
but   then   I a child   unaware—

firebrands   seared flesh   screaming pain   ships ablaze   one thou-
sand bodies blown apart eight-thousand injured   rumors of gold-
bars raining   collapsed buildings   crushing death
overturned tumblers smashed plates   cake and jelly abandoned
the party table mirrored Bombay's disaster playing out across a city
flattened   a city disappeared   a harbor in flames

my birthday evaporated
was my mother even there
if she stood beside me
if she hugged me to her
reassured it was not my wish
not my candle-breath that blew Bombay into the sky

tomorrow shall I find that nowhere
empty of noise
I've been searching if
not knowing to where
I keep going without direction

keep your hands where I can see them
blares the speed cops' megaphone

not hearing
my son   reaches inside his
jacket pocket for his
please-speak-slowly-I-am-deaf card
kerboom   too late

thoughts

no need to see what's going on
nor chatter endlessly
a rock's purpose is just to be

don't wait for stones
the desert frogs to sing
their songs to awaken you
sing now

beyond my reach

I can hear the stars tonight   he said
sitting on the edge of our bed   was it   only
yesterday   he whispered his midnight words
and   laying back   beside me
pulled the milky-way through the open window

his face   beautiful   a poem
beside me   on my pillow

today   I cup my hands   press my face   into
the grey-green waters   of his world   feel his
fingers clamp   about
my wrists   to keep from drowning

treading water   clinched
as one   we struggle in the raging waves   of
his Parkinsonian sea   to reclaim   the kingdom
he once ruled

his voice bubbles   upwards   to the surface
as I   watch   he sinks
beyond my reach

dreamtime

the magician holds a card before me
is this the word you seek he demands
this one
this

I shake my head

spreading a fan of five and twenty images
choose any one you like he leers
pushes mine into the pack
now choose another

but the cards are glued

seeing my desperate struggle
the magician laughs

that night I find a card beneath my pillow
between my nightie's cotton folds

live its one-word message

lost to retirement

I think this deserves a toast
he announced getting to his feet
dinging a knife against his beer-filled glass
we were just four friends round a table in the Pig and Whistle
thank god I've worked my final day of twenty years at Binghams
although he smiled his eyes belied his words
I saw him as a fish circling the hook he'd just escaped   but
having no direction round and round he spun

before she left

one-plain-one-pearl-one-plain-one-pearl

before she left
....the first time
I   just four
lived in India
I know she loved me
me and my baby brother
I finger the frilled snapshot
mother daughter dressed alike
mother daughter posed side by side
broadly smiling on a sunbaked rooftop
matching cardies shiny buttons down each front

why else teach me how to knit

one-plain-one-pearl-one-plain-one-pearl
needles clacking
pink stripes
kitten grey
I struggle to remember

remind myself
me and
my brother
she loved us then

wake-up call in india

the circus is coming the circus is coming
magic cargo disgorges into Sorga's dusty village square one
hot afternoon when I was six

I run with Ayah

elephant dung   rank tiger smell   sun seared cages
pink monkey fingers reach but cannot touch me
stallions too limp to swish away the flies feasting on their eyes
droop statue-still   an iron-collared Himalayan dancing-bear
strains at his chain   not dancing

can I go home now please Ayah

come evening pretty in a crisp smocked frock
fidgeting beside mummy and my little brother
I wait with white sahibs in the front row of the traveling circus tent
for drums to roll heralding the parade   for the sawdust to fill with
blaze and blare   the red-coated ringmaster's whip to crack
inches from our cushioned ringside seats

clowns   tigers   acrobats   elephants
I clap transfixed

lips gaudy red   in tinsel leotards   all at once a girl   my age
her arms as thin as mine   bends backwards   head between her legs
chin cupped in her hands   lopes towards me sideways   crab-like
eyes locked on mine   when
suddenly unwinding   she leaps   lands triumphant with a flourish
onto her father's
shoulders her eyes fixed hungrily on the pink candy floss sticky in my
hand
next moment   swinging high on a trapeze she vanished
tangling   dangling ropes   left me questioning
she was working   she wasn't having fun

midnight strikes

not quite awake   between soft sheets
I dream gold and silver treasures beneath my pillow
plates spilling food   shiny patent leather shoes
dresses   daylong play   my adoring Ayah
while
outside my fairy palace walls children
littler than me   live yoked to life's harsh lottery
no loving hand to brush shine into their hair
no sweet voice to lull them to slumber

baksheesh   they claw my arm   Ayah shoos them away
says *memsahiba I don't have any*

flamingo-philes

what is it about pink flamingoes   that just about
everybody not only loves them but   wants one

look at the flocks invading neighborhood lawns
frozen   heads down   black beaks forever grazing
plastic grass on the hunt for non-existent shrimp

I confess to cutting one from steel for myself
life-size   lobster-pink   one leg partly raised
my flamingo stands sentinel over the three goldfish
in my back garden pond where nobody sees

I fell in flamingo-love one summer sunset touring the French Camargue
when   from among the rose-pink salt hills burst a cloud of wild white
horses galloping across the marsh-flats setting off a salmon-colored flare
of beating feathered wings into the air

reminders   not that I'll forget   six magnets
fly the length of my fridge door back home
a couple of post cards too   don't tell anyone
but I am a flamingo-phile like you

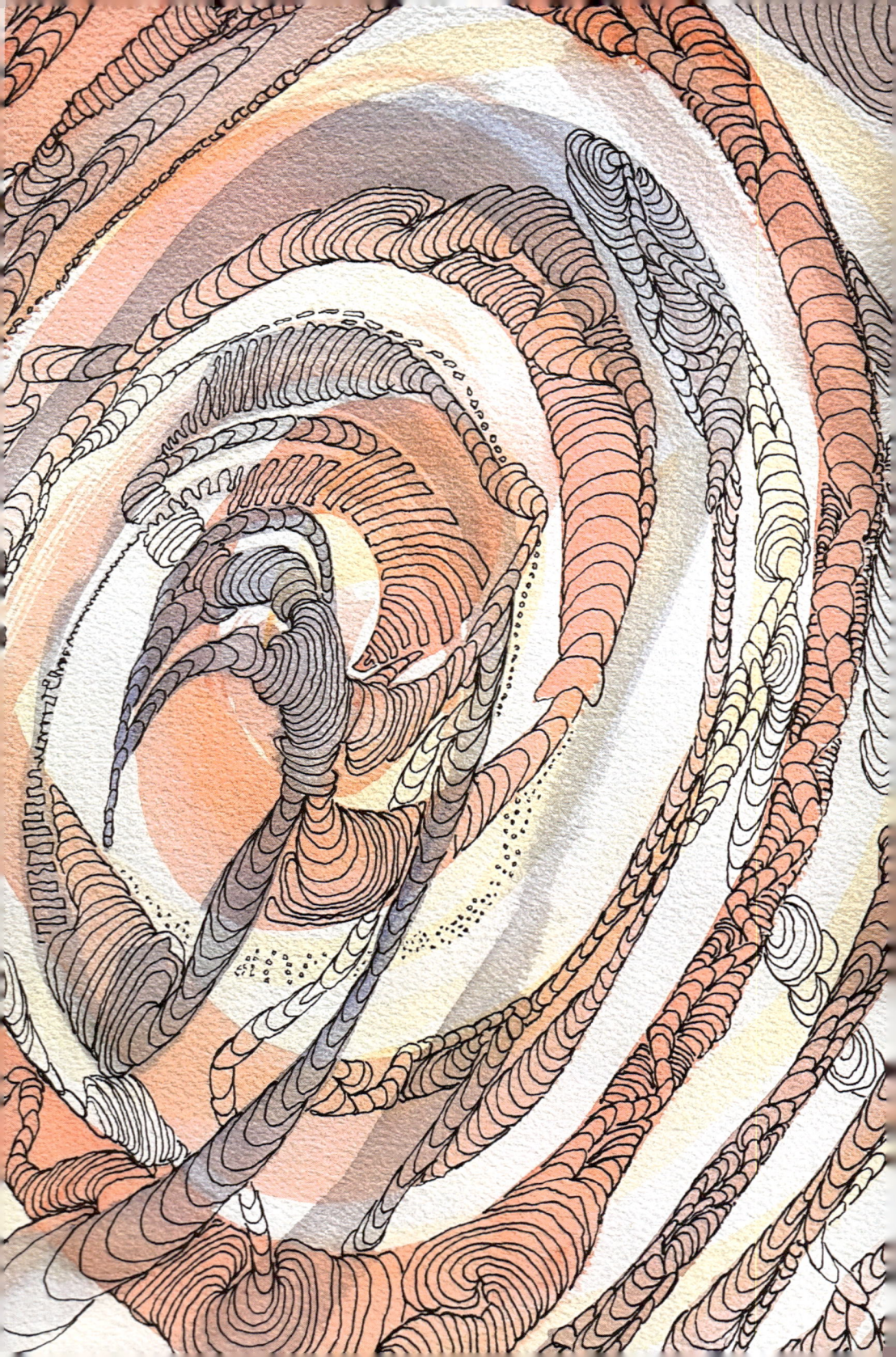

in the end is the beginning

at the top was written *do not forget*
at the bottom *goodbye forever*
not knowing what caused
him to write such a message
the page blurs indecipherable

impatient   too curious

be it novel   short-story   a letter
my nature is to begin at the end
to the who-dun-its   how-whys
the very last page reveals
which once exhumed
cannot be re-buried
only then
I read the convoluted
wanderings   the breathless
suspense of in-between words

goodbye forever

crumpling the page
tears roll undamned

a pretty curse

what a pretty girl her mother's friends exclaimed
what a pretty girl her mother's new husband leered
come sit on my lap my dear   and so liking his arms around her waist
aged six or four she did
would you mind darling putting her to bed and pouring me another gin her
mother cajoled extending her martini glass *I'm quite worn out today*

my friend Sandra's face turned ugly remembering the bedtime stories she'd
been told never   not ever   ever share

at college then grown and living alone   she fell pregnant   expelled to scrub
floors at a home for wayward girls never to hold her new born   never
cradle her baby

sent to live with a friend of her mother's   he thought her pretty too   hands
wandering he smiled
a crocodile smile   *what a pretty girl you are my dear   let me introduce you to
my friends*   they thought her pretty too

did you want to sleep with all those dirty men I asked
not really she replied   *but they wanted it   and paid to have a boob job*
eventually she married   still hoping to find love

last dance

let's dance he whispers
pulls me to my feet

scarcely moving
fingers lightly interlaced
we dance together one last time
to a long-forgotten tune

though snow lies on the ground
apple blossom scents his breath

cheek soft against his chest
chin gentle on my head
I relive our first kiss
waltzed across the ballroom floor

just following orders

I caught a scorpion
hiding in my clothes
swept him into a screw-top jar as
instructed by my landlord

to this day
I cringe   ashamed not
of capturing it
of keeping him captive
ten long days and nights
it took
before
defeated
it blackened

to this day
I see him
bravely
poised to strike
stinger ready
above his head

wake up sweating at the pearly gates
I caused a creatures suffering

journey to silence

my first day
startled awake by songs of Jesus bellowed
from the battery of loudspeakers strung palm tree
to palm tree in the church gardens over the wall

Sunday   of course
India   of course   where silence is hard to find
sermon prayers and psalms follow in Malayalam
a tongue strange to my ears
not once   not twice   no   three two-hour services
5-7am   7-9   9-11

the preacher at last falling wordless
clouds of screeching crow-like birds take
over celebrating day without pause
till mosquitoes take wing at dusk
keep your cool   keep your cool   mad
mad   we'll send you mad   their buzzing whines

retreating to the tic-a-tock   slowly spinning blades
the ceiling fan above my bed
t-omorrow   t-omorrow   t-omorrow will come they strum as I fall
asleep to terrifying scenarios from not my life but a life-time I hope

never to have lived   march into   then exit my brain

day dawns   no passing storm   ten of twenty nights   days
ear-pounding rain strikes coconuts   batters palms fronds to
the ground   blurs   blank   my world beyond four walls
trick or real   I'm not sure   a low *om om* intrudes   from
within monsoon's   beating   drumming   see
the day security guard   perched   stack of daybeds beneath
the stairwell   the watery curtain wall stringing earth to sky

eyes closed   deep in communication with his divine
om om   vibrating with each breath

aware suddenly of his great wealth of spirit   contentment
my lack   humbled   I bow   see before me
a man in touch with his soul
messenger   teacher   silently   thank him

just me   singing frogs in the lotus pool
sodden tubs of potted herbs outside my room
I hear music playing in the deluge
discover the other body of mine
that reveals itself through stillness

I pass the day at peace with isolation
practice the art of stillness
discover where it is I have to go

on the lee side of the mountain
man leaves no shadow

your face
beside me on my pillow
a love poem

jellied eels her brain
abandoned by family
where am I she pleads

thoughts

beneath skin's surface
deeper than my bones
a string of pearls

a lone fruit blushes
red among green apple
leaves
withers uneaten

yellow

"Mine is a beautiful shield. There is yellow pollen in it." Momaday

always imaging the worst
never feeling   one of them
them   being a group that is

it's just not safe
to reveal the gold
inside the jacket I keep
tightly buttoned   that   once loosened
might   like clouds of yellow pollen release
into the air alongside migrating spiders newly hatched
each trailing an incandescent filament

emptiness is just a space for light

I know you think I've forgotten where last your fingers lay
I slide my hand into the mattress indent you once filled
allow a tear fall

though a hundred years may pass
a hundred dawns flare and fade
I still remember

live wildly
make love   skip and play   hold hands
I want to scream to every passing couple
for today will become tomorrow's memory

when next you lie together   before the other's waking
breathe in rhythm with your beloved's softly ballooning cheeks
trace each laugh line of your lover's face
tickle open each eyelid with parted lips

though a hundred dawns may flare and fade
remembering I'll smile
knowing emptiness is just a space for light
and what we shared is what we'd spent lifetimes seeking

night search

arms stretched fumbling night's dense rectangle open doorway I take a step

I am hunting for the woman with the crooked tooth who
never shared my growing   never saw me   the lopsided teenager mooning her
image through lipstick I-love-you hearts scrawled across
the mirror glass

I want to find her grieving

I am hunting for the woman whose hand once gently guided my pencil
scribed the letters *e-l-i-z-a-b-e-t-h and m-u-m-m-y*
drew me a long-eared bunny with a star-shaped tail   watched me add spiked
whiskers

I want to find her on her knees   weeping   beside the collapsed house
of cards   ten stories high   red diamond homes   we built together but never
shared   it is the knave of spades she holds   death's card   she pulls me to her
plants a kiss

I want her to see me vainly waiting   she's not there

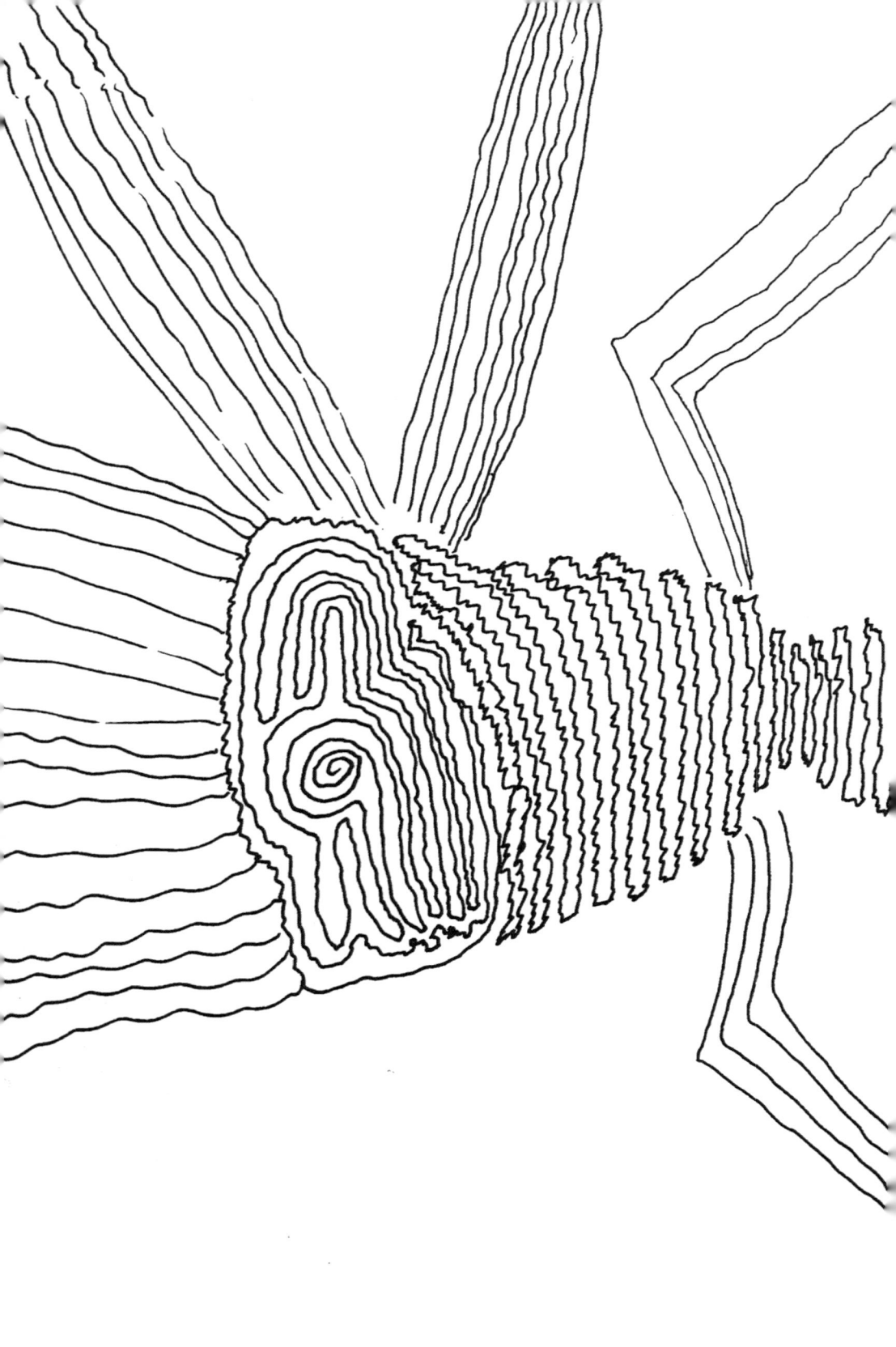

a bad day

I should have stayed in bed
when
my electric toothbrush battery failed
when
a dawn telephone call disturbed
when
my coffee cup crashed from the table knocked by a careless swipe
hungry
the fridge held one rotting lettuce   some stale cheese
and
the film highly priced we drove twenty-five miles to see
a lengthy drag interspersed with secondhand coughs and sneezes
what kind of a date are you I sneered
when
he moved one seat away leaving me alone to give himself more legroom
when
eyes closed he snored
I should never have left my bed that day

why should they get it

it's no fun growing old
tweezers searching grabbing the rogue
overnight hair sprouting from my chin
no fun at all scurrying to make it to the
street's far side before the flashing green
walk countdown   3-2-1 seconds ends
and   the tidal wave of tooting cars blare
out of the way   doddering old fool

no   the young just don't get
some things are just no longer
possible   nor why should they
not their time

I mean things like grab-bar-less showers
exiting the sea without a strangers help
sliding down an arroyo incline too steep
from which to clamber back   on a hike
I've hiked a hundred times or more

out of the question
settling onto the ground

to contemplate awhile
the field of silver grasses
cholla skeletons back-lit
by the setting sun
no way to get back up you see

a whistle
about my neck hangs ready
hopeful someone understands
my ••• – – – •••   S.O.S. blasts

forget fall buttons
tossing in my sleep   yoga exercises   set the damn things
off raise my blood pressure to heart-attack levels in my
panic to cancel the army of flashing lights
the sirens wailing their way to drag me from my home   god
the embarrassment   god the shame   today episodes to laugh
about but not too hard   not at my age
but that's another matter

mind you offered seats   pre-boarding   airport wheelchairs   bag-carry-
ing and *may-I-help-yous*
I never refuse   might as well enjoy what few benefits there are to
growing old   and   oh yes
free food at my local senior center

I have a question

a bell in a jar won't ring
are you sure I question tap the glass
strain for the muffled thunk within

beyond the open window
a linnet's song evaporates
and in its place
the sound of cow bells
from the alpine meadow

not fit for a dog
for all those immigrants and those incarcerated

I too would howl
if   solitary   like you   I
lived chained inside a crate

where   no light
separates day from night

where   wordless
three times a day

plates of food shoved through
a metal hatch keeps you alive

daily dragged
outside into the burning sun
orange as your jumpsuit

walk   fifty minutes
in a treeless desert pen
far from home

where
looking skyward
infinity   reminds

not a dog
you are a human
you are a sentient being

wolves in sheep's clothing....
the village rodeo parade

nothing changing but our graying hair
the increased caverns between our loosening teeth
the cracking of arthritic joints
with sinking heart I approach the crowded portal
each year to watch the rodeo parade

brims pulled low
a pack of wolves in cowboy hats
hungry for my bones eye me   their next quarry
come closer they entice   blowing air kisses
through plastic smiles   query
not caring one way or the other
another year gone
hi how've you been

my she's aged
how thin she's become
wrinkled too poor thing
their thinking screams aloud

my what big teeth you have my dears
I silently return
politely smiling back

the village fire truck whoop-whoops into view
heralding the parade
hurrah hurrah we wave
hurrah hurrah we cheer

politics gone mad

when the sea turned red   has the world turned upside down   I questioned
I did a handstand and discovered that indeed it had   and I paddled between
white berries growing in the sea   collected fifty-two and strung them in a
glittering coil about my neck   who am I to know which way is up which way
is down   it's all a game   the rules of which are hidden in   the sky   or is it the
sea   both of which are blazing

I have my life back

after
hands white-knuckled on the wheel weaving mobius loops across the center
line to the verge
he hung his car keys on a hook

after
arcing a Jackson Pollock minestrone from his spoon across a restaurant's wall
he ate at home

after
suffering a parkinson's freeze in the cinema's doorway blocking the audience
from exiting
movies limited to home TV

after
one bitch-woman tapped his shoulder at a concert yelling *keep your head still
God dammit*
he confined himself in solitary

after
tremoring jig-sawed letters on the printed page   books stayed shelved unread
he gave his kindle to a friend
life is not worth living if I have to live this way he wept

until
electrodes were planted in his brain

bionic
he tapped the battery in his chest
I have my life back he sang
it was true and sang the words again

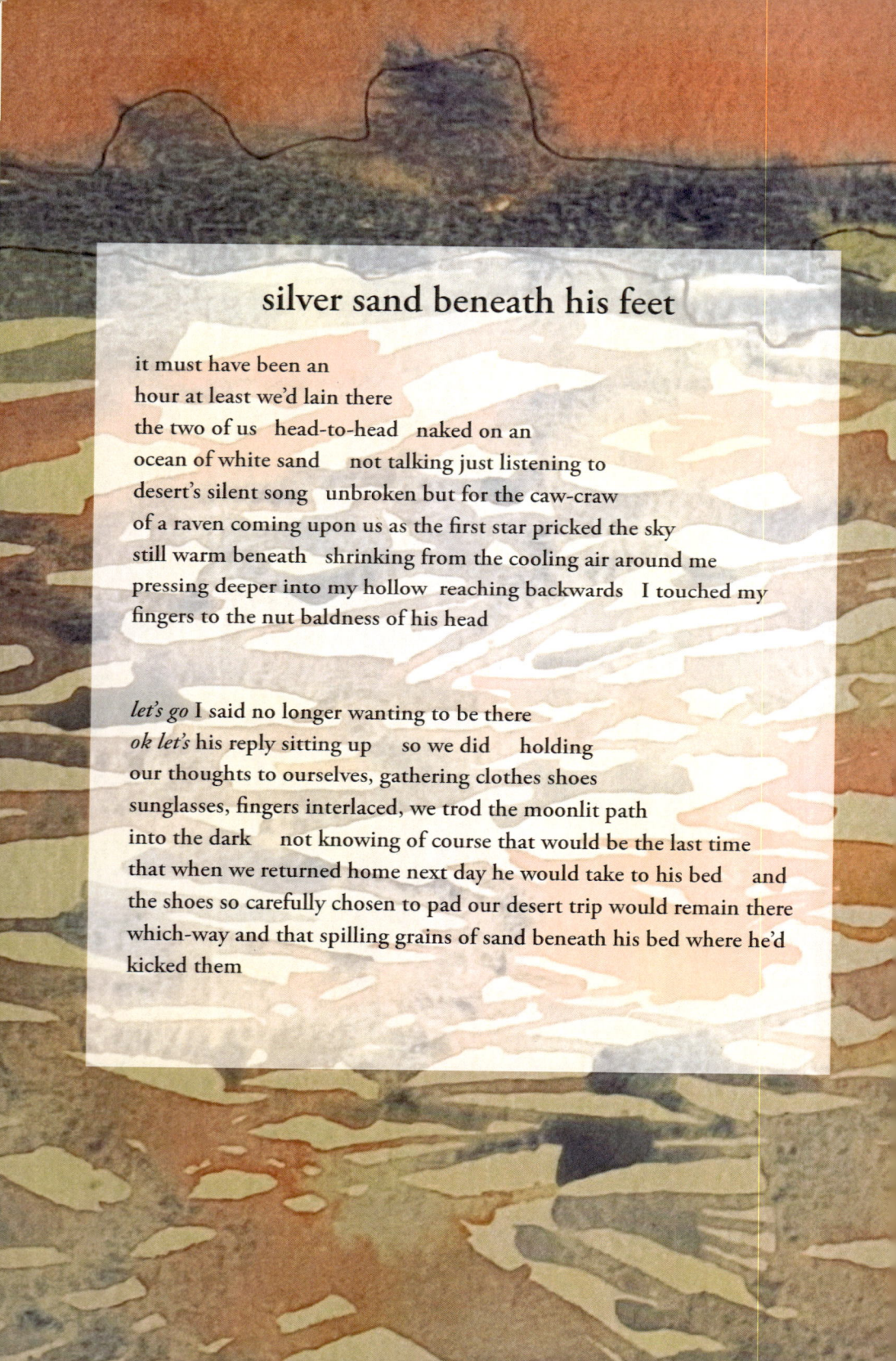

silver sand beneath his feet

it must have been an
hour at least we'd lain there
the two of us   head-to-head   naked on an
ocean of white sand   not talking just listening to
desert's silent song   unbroken but for the caw-craw
of a raven coming upon us as the first star pricked the sky
still warm beneath   shrinking from the cooling air around me
pressing deeper into my hollow reaching backwards   I touched my
fingers to the nut baldness of his head

let's go I said no longer wanting to be there
ok let's his reply sitting up   so we did   holding
our thoughts to ourselves, gathering clothes shoes
sunglasses, fingers interlaced, we trod the moonlit path
into the dark   not knowing of course that would be the last time
that when we returned home next day he would take to his bed   and
the shoes so carefully chosen to pad our desert trip would remain there
which-way and that spilling grains of sand beneath his bed where he'd
kicked them

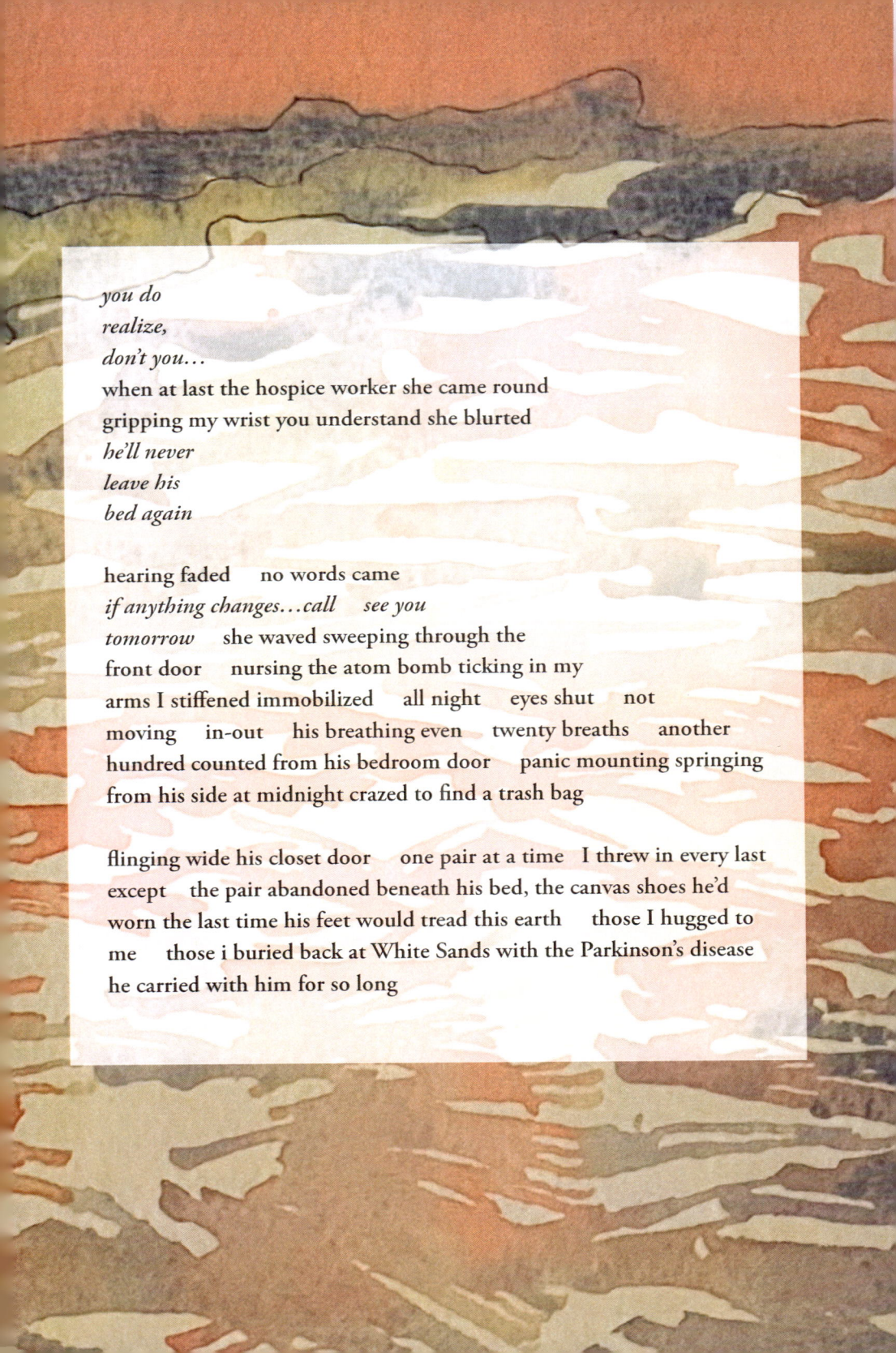

you do
realize,
don't you…
when at last the hospice worker she came round
gripping my wrist you understand she blurted
he'll never
leave his
bed again

hearing faded   no words came
if anything changes…call   *see you*
tomorrow   she waved sweeping through the
front door   nursing the atom bomb ticking in my
arms I stiffened immobilized   all night   eyes shut   not
moving   in-out   his breathing even   twenty breaths   another
hundred counted from his bedroom door   panic mounting springing
from his side at midnight crazed to find a trash bag

flinging wide his closet door   one pair at a time   I threw in every last
except   the pair abandoned beneath his bed, the canvas shoes he'd
worn the last time his feet would tread this earth   those I hugged to
me   those i buried back at White Sands with the Parkinson's disease
he carried with him for so long

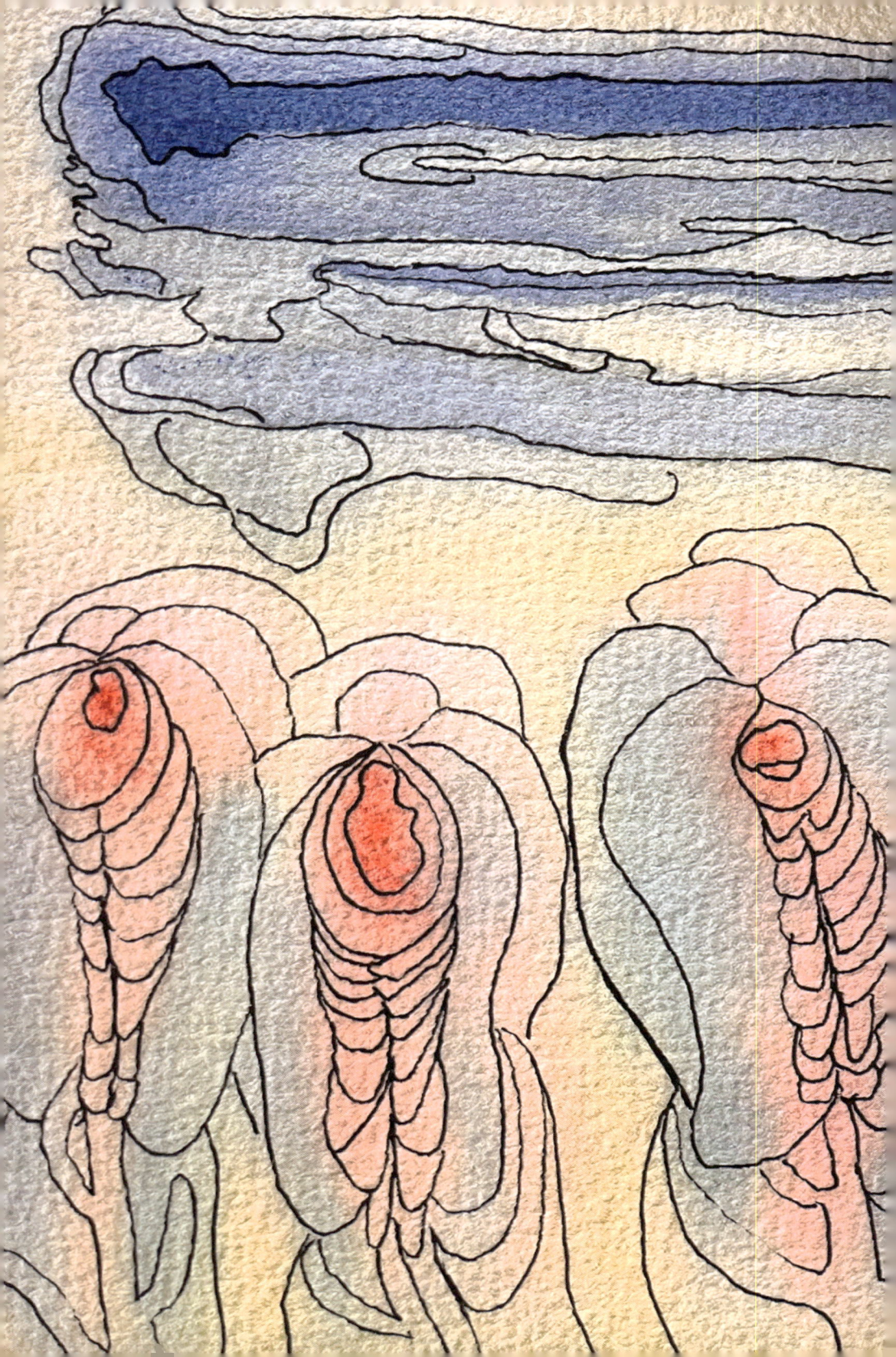

six years a widow

it's a beautiful day today
I belt out full volume

so used to silence the walls tremble
and whatever I have to do...

flinging my arms to the empty room
I dance the space awake

it's a lovely day for doing it that's true
loud words crowd the house with song

waking
missing noise
somedays
I bang the kettle to its base
relish the explosive rattle-clatter
bubbling ritual making of my early morning tea
the chink of spoon and cup disturbing dawn's feather quiet

outside the kitchen window
scudding clouds wisp apart
revealing sky's forever pageant
and   to be alive is still beautiful

listening for your return

seeking you
each morning
ear pressed against your door
straining for the slow shuffle-scrape
your slippers etch across the flagstone floor
fearing a hollow echo   I hesitate
before
letting drop
the brass knocker
we chose together
before
without a word you vanished   that
thursday evening two long months ago
cobwebs bind shut the windows
shield the yellowed tablecloth
our two places   expectant
on the kitchen table
no aromatic vapor
escapes the iron casserole
its half-moon handle
smooth from years of lifting
hangs cold   lifeless   on the hob
each visit   the cottage sinks   and
I must bend lower to part its ivy tendrils
did a blackberry vine tumble you into the river
sweep you downstream   face   turned hawk-ward
to the gold hidden in the sun
come my love
I obey your whisper
rest my axe against the wall   stack Pinon
newly cut
in the willow basket
I wove for you last winter

widow's rings and loss

come back to me or I will surely perish   three nights   dusk to daybreak
 a woman's anguished cries pit the shoreline beneath the fullness of the moon

ghostly in her nightgown   weeping   wildly pulling at her hair
the mourner calls to her lost soul   searches ocean's tangled detritus
discarded widows' rings   herringbones   glistening strands of kelp
maniacal in her madness the woman troils the foaming surf
thrashes the shallow waters   deaf to the receding tide's mocking hiss
your soul is now mine I own that which you lost

at last   she cackles   *got you*
she lunges at a passing shoal slippering between and about her toes
catches up three fish   holds fast their heads between her teeth
stops her grieving

a single aster
a pool of fallen leaves
a sign of autumn

in the absence of the moon
stars show their brilliance

more thoughts

from a mountain peak
the only way to go is down
from its base the only way is up

up the path and down again

where are you going
a neighbor's call
pauses me in my daily walking
I wave towards the attic window from which she leans
so where was I going
from nowhere to nowhere my answer

his story: and who is crazy

1980's prison riot   santa fe
one of the psychiatrists on call
years later my friend held me with his tale

for your protection
all I'll say   is   31 panicked prisoners
their guards   died unspeakable deaths
seared images I'm unable to erase

his face sagged
loving him   reached for his hand
so   his voice faltered
so   he continued

I couldn't work after what
I'd seen   after what I heard

CLOSED INDEFINITELY
I nailed the notice to my office door
packed two bags   roamed the world
Hawaii   Morocco   Malaysia
a beach-bum   I surfed the pounding seas
sucked ripe oranges   smoked a little weed
sat Buddha-like beneath a coconut palm

my fingers trailing silver grain

two years and all but a few dollars gone   still
I hesitated   not yet ready to return home
not yet empty inside my head   got myself
hired by a government-run psyche clinic
in big apple's sunless shadowland

cold metal desk   grey office walls
grey as the temp work I undertook
where   doc-only elevators cocooned
their staff   isolated the whitecoats from
the desperate they were employed to help
street people smell   staff members sniffed

one day my first month I called an ambulance
committed a raving patient to bedlam
protect him from self-harm

curious to see the infamous hospital
curious   if the wards were   as
shocking as rumor claimed
I called by at the end of the day

I am a doctor I announced
here to see my client

security security
the receptionist backed away
the wail of sirens alarmed
helmeted   guns ready
four guards surrounded
handcuffed my wrists
frog-marched me away

taking my watch my belt my shoes
threw me in a holding cell for hours
for impersonating a doctor they accused
for never before
no   not once   not ever   had a doctor
checked up on his client in person

imprisoned by grey
back in my office
NY's winter wind
whipped my bones

I dreamed big sky
unbroken desert horizons
new mexico   home

whitewash the walls
splash sunshine into this miserable hole
I instructed two homeless clients   one yawning weekend

I'll pay you well

monday
rainbows arced the window sill
daffodils scarlet poinsettias   trailing spider plants
wonder lit every client's and clinician's face
but one

remembering   my doctor friend smiled

tight-lipped the medical director spat
redecoration is against regulations
I order you
re-paint the walls back as they were grey

paint them yourself lady
I hereby resign
ripping off my badge
threw it and my keys to the floor
forcing bitch-boss to grovel at my feet
you're fired   her screech came too late
already through the door I was gone and far away

and who is the prisoner and who is crazy
my friend laughed as he ended his tale

you were already beautiful my darling

before
the surgeon stretched taught your skin
before
your oh so-soft lips and breasts ballooned bubblegum tight
I feared they'd pop
before
your laugh   your worry lines   were erased

I miss the crows' feet   your furrowed frown   your slant-eyed stare
the etched life-stories in your face that held your beauty

expect no praise from me
when   doll-like you return
with your cookie-cutter face
your body skeletal

you were already beautiful my darling

once a king

today   every day   I cup my hands   press my face into
the grey-green waters   his world   feel   his   fingers
clamp my wrists   keep from drowning   treading water
clinched   struggle the raging waves   of   his
Parkinsonian sea   reclaim the kingdom   he once ruled

hold on my love
I'm here
I cry

flotsam   garbled   my voice bubbles   to the surface
watch him sink
beyond my reach

…when a photo from a winter ten years ago spread a memory across my
computer screen   I cried   the two of us   king   queen   snapped pull-
ing silly faces outside the Pompidou   Paris   waggling fingers   gloved
thumbs   frozen in our ears   Miro   Matisse icicles shining in the iris of
our eyes   I'd forgotten how firm his skin   how vibrant our coupling   I
crumpled unable to dam my tears

life sentence

your sentence
life without parole
you are to be taken from here to
a secure place to serve out your term
pardon   for which my Susan pleaded   *refused*

I grip the steering wheel
pass through iron gates
park   enter reception
the inner door is locked

four years have passed
hers between four walls
mine spread continents
a smattering of Japanese learned from Duolingo

I ring the bell   wait
visiting   *Susan*
time   *10.15*
sign in   *Liz*   I scrawl my name

keys turned
bolts being drawn
crash me to the present

yes a voice queries
I'm here to see Susan I say

find her
eyes closed
nestled with a clutch
of other white-haired inmates
waiting for the one-eyed ogre blaring
from the wall to cease its relentless barrage
to keep your skin youthful...wrinkle free
a lip-sticked blonde plugs beauty tips
unaware on whose ears her garbage falls

five faces turn   tentative   wordless   plead
me   have you come to visit me   me
for a second twenty eyes sparkle
will I be it   the chosen one

pale cheeks firm   hopeful smiles   sag as I pass
not you   not you   you   I stop   point
as in the children's game *lucy-locket*
Susan lifts her head

scrape   lift   clunk
scrape-clunk   rubber tips   green linoleum
her walker inches headed for her room
young   old   slowly we walk

half way she rests
hawks   splat
saliva hits the wall

Susan
I bite my lip
you can't do that
shhh   don't tell
she sniggers
her eyes light up

my room   she smiles
quick   shut the door
I help Susan settle on
the embroidered
scarlet posy of
poppies cushioning her chair

I'm 99 you know
eyelids fluttering
lies adds two years
briefly her head sinks
snail-like from the baby-blue blouse of her shell   uncurls
how lovely to see you darling   where is it you live now   her face
brightens
mother   daughter   we clasp hands   squeeze
petal soft   rough bark
you're really here   deep pools   her eyes hold mine   we swim

questions   answers repeat   words circle fresh as if
spoken for the first time

I read to her
her own story
unfold her life from within two sheets of paper written years before
the story she wants read at her funeral

Susan Sclater born 1914 The Close Hampshire
torpedoed…I never knew my Admiral father…became a Red Cross
nurse…tent camp… Algeria…bandaged wounded troops…ordered to
Anzio…no map…drove a ten-ton- lorry…my friend Joyce and I… so
cold…stitched woolen skirts from army blankets…

really   I did all those things   memories ramble
you remember Wuzzer my terrier don't you Liz
it was before my time I whisper

five six seven times and yet again I read aloud
Susan drinks in every word till finally she's sated

goodbye   I kiss her   forehead   both cheeks
Susan never looks up   I leave her room weeping

in the corridor
outside her door a woman clutches at my sleeve

help   I need help   please   please   I should be home
perhaps you can tell me
what am I doing I here

life pearl

I need only look beneath the surface of my skin
peer deeper than my bones to find the glistening
pearl kept hidden there   hold for a precious
moment in my palm   remind life
glows beautiful